The Universe for Breakfast

Sharon

THE UNIVERSE FOR BREAKFAST

Dharma Diary Poems

by

JOY MAGEZIS

BLACK
APOLLO
PRESS

To the Dads –
Marty Magezis & Ed Biderman
To the Moms –
Florence Magezis & Fannie Biderman
To the ancestors
back through time
interconnected
to essence of life

To new generations
and those yet to come
out through space
interwoven
through boundless universe

In gratitude
for being alive
to experience all this

First published in Great Britain by Black Apollo Press, 2007
Copyright © Joy Magezis 2007

The moral right of the author has been asserted.

A CIP catalogue record of this book is available at the
British Library.

ISBN: 9781900355551

CONTENTS

INTRODUCTION

Eight years ago
back from holiday
to write my novel
a poem appeared
Then this flood

What lies beyond?
Journey begun
with the help
of great teachers
family and friends

Finding way
through thickets
of suffering
fear undergrowth
dazzling joy

Unimagined path
to tread life
each very instant
Dharma my guide
I make my own way

Dear friend
I invite you to share
my inner heart life
Perhaps it will help
on your own way

7 January 2007, Cambridge, UK

*Dharma is the teachings of the Buddha and those
who followed along the path of understanding and love.*

27 September 1998

I.

The sun,
shining through the trees,
crosses my heart.
It brings the warmth
I so desire.
Igniting the light within.

Touching my fear with comfort,
focusing my essence on growth.
The light,
shining through the trees,
is part of me.

II.

Droplets fall from the leaves.
And the fields echo
with the thumps of horses' hoofs.
As they run out their restlessness,
I touch my own with comfort
and hold my fear with understanding.

I, too, can find peace
in interconnection,
for I am horses, rain and sun.
All of these are my precious life.
And the hoof-beats echoing within
resound with my longing
to know what lies hidden.

Beyond my vulnerability
there is a great sun
which I want to be.
It shines through the branches of my fear
and lights the glen beyond.

9 November 1998

Love, Light Grow.
Fear, Guilt Go.
Go with my blessing.
No anger left
just faith
in this very moment.

Hold that faith.
Shine that love
into my very depths.
Spaces so dark
they cringe
to be recognised.
Places I've dared
not touch
for fear of spreading
deadly poison.

But I need not fear.
I will not drown
in my own poison.
Fear expanded it.
The light shows
only droplets
awaiting transformation.

How simple it sounds.
But it takes
that leap
to a new dimension.
Diving into
intuitive love.

From that place long forgotten,
denied, abandoned,
comes a wish
for the crystal
to refract such light
as I didn't know was there.

A rainbow appears
shaking the caverns
of my very doubt.
'And you ain't
seen nothing yet.'

Suddenly I draw back
in terror of the jinx
who will twist my words
of blasphemy.
Knock on wood
quickly before it hears
I shall worship fear again.

NO!
I'm scared,
but I'll go anyway.
Into my rainbow,
softening my heart
blessing my fear
remembering that –
I am worthy of love.

17 November 1998

FEAR NOT WRITING

Fear not this writing
from true heart.
Ask not its meaning.
Take the insights and live.
For life is but a flash.
And you can only
live each instant
when there is no time
so you live forever.

Fear not your own words.
Don't censor them.
They will not ruin you.
They are not evil
or discordant.
Your words are perfect
if you trust them.

Fear not
the imaginary tiger within.
Those depths are holy places
disguised as dungeons.
Fear has veiled them in pain.
When disrobed
the sun will shine in.

Fear not
what others will say
or their judgements.
Needn't write for them.
Forget them behind you,
wagging their fingers.
Forget their echoes within.
(Or is it the other way round?)

Fear not being selfish.
You can only love yourself
if you want to be able
to truly love others.
Love self.
Write for self
and the river of love will flow
with golden light.

Forget to limit you
and the ocean within
will break lose
and flow through
your fingertips.

Fear not
the white waves breaking,
as they did at the start of labour,
giving birth to art.
Trust your own muse.
She will not harm you,
if you are receptive
to your true self.

Perhaps I could
write like this forever.
If I feared not
what came out.
Some would be useful.
Some later deleted.
But how purifying
just to sit before the keys
with my eyes closed
and let my fingers
bring the words
from my mind
to the page.

No time limit.
No audience.
Suspending judgement
just smiling at the chance
to flow.
The thrill
of being ART.

For art is process
unbounded, uncritical.
Expressing my soul,
exposing my inner depths,
uncaring of product.
From this groundswell
seeping up
from what I thought
was the deepest sewers
comes ME.

22 November 1998

CHANUKAH

Changing seasons.
Darkening light.
Chanukah approaching.
Family gathering.

And I miss you, Mom.
You who recreated
holiday lights
in the darkness.
Feeling so deeply
the vacuum left
without Christmas.
Reaching back
for that heritage
bursting with light.

Thank you, Mom
for making Chanukah
so wondrously bright.
— For the latkes,
cray paper decorations,
origami dradles,
you taught us to make.

Thank you for helping me
be proud of my culture,
beyond religion, oppression,
self hate, aggrandisement.

Focusing on positive,
with meaning for us,
creating the holiday
you longed for as a child.

And most of all
thank you, Mom,
for your shining love.

WINTER CONNECTIONS

Energy at my scalp,
beyond headache,
branching out
from the boundaries
of what seems to be
ME.

I can sense
the branches
that protrude
out from my scalp
in all directions
to the very edge
of bare bark.
There sprigs await spring,
beyond fear, disbelief.

Tara, so sure,
sitting on windowsill
with the big, old tree
beyond the glass.
And me,
on my cushion,
trying to follow suit.

I am sure.
I feel
those branches
growing
from my backbone
out to my potential,
beyond understanding
to faith, wisdom.

I feel those branches
growing from the pain
in my back
transforming it
to lightness and warmth.
Bringing me to the very edge.

Here in the depths of winter
those bare branches
sustain energy,
deepening mine
to go beyond.

Out on the spread of branches
birds roost awaiting spring,
without need of explanation.
Out there I want to fly
with my birds.

Wings expanded,
large black birds
soar on currents
of winter winds,
without being cold.
Inner warmth protects,
spurring them on.

Beyond the birds
lie streaks
of white clouds,
holding the sky
in their winter mist.

I am the haze
of moisture
which stripes the blueness
with its life-giving water.

Beyond the clouds
I am white snow
which begins to fall
as tiny dots
building to heavy clumps.
I feel the force
drifting to earth
with ever increasing ferocity
until finally
it covers the land.

I am the earth
deep and strong
covered with snow
brimming with life.
I am the earth,
as I sit
on my cushion,
kneeling on blanket
crocheted by Mom.
We are the earth –
life itself.

Grounded,
I feel energy
against my shins.
The heat, beyond snow,
works its way
up my body.
I see the redness
and feel my scalp,
expanding out
into branches,
growing ever stronger,
connections.

19 January 1999

Waking to image
of spiritual woman.
Her glistening, white hair
standing up on end -
an electric crown.

Electricity, too,
extending out
her finger tips.
Her arms spread,
palms upward,
welcoming me.

She stands tall,
body contentedly full,
legs apart,
feet touching earth.

Her aura is rainbow,
invitingly beautiful,
shining toward me.
But I can't help
being scared.

'Are wise women scared?'
Her smile grows wider,
'My old friend fear.
Such good energy
once transformed.'
'But how?'
'By not allowing
fear to block you.
There's so much more.
It's merely a trifle.'

From her heart
a golden light
eases my fear.
Now I see
her third eye
brightly coloured
across her forehead.

My concentration deeper,
I notice her round
belly stone,
dark and heavy,
grounding her.

She wears a long,
multi-coloured coat.
In it I find
possibilities abound.

6 February 1999

RELEASE THE JEW

I

Release from bondage
so deep a fear
scared of evil
the Holocaust
witnessed by my people
victims of Auschwitz

Release from bondage
of subterranean belief
in the power of evil
touch wood against
the evil eye
for we so vulnerable
to death and fear

Release from bondage
of inner fear
that I, too, contain
the potential to inflict
torture and death
That I, too, could
be a party to genocide

Release from bondage
the deep fear
that within me lies
tiger of destruction
if unleashed
anger and hurt
would cause me
to be evil

Release from bondage
the deadly power
of pain, the spin
of negative force
before my birth
that I arose
out of energy
of the Holocaust

I am the rebirth
of those who died
screaming in gas chambers
horror vibrating
over and over
millions upon millions
Bodies looted for gold fillings
burnt in open trenches
the stench of mass death
polluting the earth

Release from bondage
for I am more
than the terrible deaths
More than the evil
which caused them
For 'evil' is merely
a human construct
of fear and pain
poison spun
into hurt and anger
manifested in
human destruction

Release from bondage
for I am also
the earlier life
of Holocaust victims
before rounded up
packed into cattle cars
humiliated and murdered
I am their music
their art, their theories,
their hopes and dreams
I am their future

Release from bondage
my fear of becoming
the devil of evil
my people witnessed
I am their hope
their love of life
Heart opening
I discover not evil
but pain and hurt
fear and death
creativity, energy
deep abiding love

Release from bondage
I need not copy
destructive energy
of the persecutor
Even Israel
when it persecutes
the Palestinians
is not me.

II

Released from bondage
I'm amazed to find
I'm the shining light
compassion of Tara
potential of growth
generosity, warmth
Suspicion itself
my fear of depths
is the very lock
holding from release
that storehouse of energy
of those who've gone
of what I am
What I can become

Released from bondage
opened to universe
the source of love
vibrating orange
yellow and green
Life itself
purple of spirit
heat of success
touch of energy
flowing through fingers
conscious breathing
balancing aura

Released from bondage
mistaken self-hate
misguided suspicion
maintenance of 'evil'
for they are but
the spinning of fire
in the wrong direction
That energy released
can cool, transform
as I can become
a daughter of light

Beyond bondage
of biblical stories
of Jewish slaves
the power of God
suppresser of Goddess
who are but one
All forms of love
separated by religion
contain the essence
to guide us all
Compassion and hope
faith and openness
await me now

Beyond my habit
to brace for evil
expect the worst
fear the devil
hear the screams
of horrific torture
Scares –
seemingly unhealable
nightmares suppressed
and taken in
turned on one's self
turned on others

To fear's manifestations
with deep compassion
for all its victims
I send my love
protecting my heart
with translucent shell
allowing positivity
to permeate out
for all who suffer

19 February 1999

In deep meditation
I contacted ancestors
who told me they wanted
me to transform
all their suffering

Opening my eyes
in shock, despair
so much darkness
such heavy weight
Impossible job

Once calm I returned
to ancestral connection
and they said,
'Ve just vant
 you should be happy'

19 March 1999

SPRING TRANSFORMATION

*I gave this poem to my teacher,
Thich Nhat Hanh, who is a Zen
Master and peace activist. It was
part of my letter asking to take the
5 Mindfulness Trainings. They are
an expanded, insightful version of
the 5 Buddhist precepts. After the
transmission ceremony, Thay (the
Vietnamese word for 'teacher')
gave me the Lineage Name of
Restoring Life of the Heart. At the
time I was surprised that the
name sounded like that of a healer.*

In light green dress,
floor length
I stand, legs spread,
surrounded by grass
growing longer
aglow with sun.

Atop high red mountain,
arms lifted
touching sky
feet grounded,
limbs form an 'x'.
Belly, my core,
I breath
and breath.

I am
the green
sprig of growth –
life itself,
photosynthesis,
charge of electric
impulse splattering
across time
to this very moment
when life
sprouts forth
beyond old growth
and I become
anew.

This poem was inspired by Thich Nhat Hanh's Retreat.

5 April 1999

THE UNIVERSE FOR BREAKFAST

Looking into
my cereal bowl
I find
the universe, smiling.
Banana –
from the Caribbean;
rich soil,
mother of growth
for wide-leafed tree.
Tropical rains,
cooling thirsty earth,
born of clouds,
bringing water
from distant lands
to the buds,
ready to flower.
Sun, kissing
the petals opened.

Grape Nuts cereal –
brown, ripened fields
of wheat and barley
swaying in the winds
of America's bounty.
Country of my birth
loved, with mixed emotions,
sad at your misused might
thankful for the refuge
of my desperate ancestors.

Pumpkin seeds –
from far off China,
soil for Indian wisdom
of wandering Nuns
bringing tofu and love,
germinating kernels
of Zen simplicity.

Sesame seeds –
from Guatemala,
land of hope
and death squads,
repression and
Liberation Theology.

May the sweat
upon these seeds
be repaid with
just bounty,
giving child labourers
a place at school,
full bellies and
warmth of home.

Organic milk –
from British cows
like those I see
beyond my window
munching spring growth
on Stourbridge Common,
leaving fertiliser.
All the same
to mother earth,
great transformer
of putrid smells
into rosehip buds
for next year's tea.

Sitting at my table
I taste the sweetness
of childhood food,
feeling distant products
transforming within.
Suddenly, they are real,
beyond plastic packaging
divorced from storms,
deep roots and light.

Even a city girl,
raised in cement,
can taste the universe,
chew the wind,
digest the sun
and know
it's all possible
at this very instant
when I breath,
beyond time/space,
in the ultimate dimension.

Written during the bombing of Belgrade

23 April 1999

UNIVERSAL SUNSET

Light blue streaks
in darkening sky.
Traces of light
brightening my spirit.
Pervading this moment,
if I only notice.
Nature, so patient,
beyond my worries –
despair of War,
demonstrating
we all come
to our time
in wider context
where life breaths easy
and beauty abounds.

I contact that light
in growing darkness.
An ordinary sunset
radiates insight
that sky surrounds,
even bombing strife,
with endless potential,
uniting all life,
beyond space/time,
in harmony essence.
Igniting desire
to become
agents of peace.

30 August 1999

SEWING UP THIS NEED

Deep in my dream
coming through to me
fear of separation
need to be loved

Not to be alone
I'm busy taking care
of others so that
they'll be there for me

'Come on you guys
don't leave me all alone'
But at night
when I slip into dreams
there's no one to protect me
No one can sleep in my mind
No one can comfort me
No one but me

So in my dream
I slowly sew up
the torn edges
of my fear

That rip keeps me awake
Sleepless nights
the mantra of my life
Always fear
of being alone
losing control
of conscious mind

Fear stalks
to keep me awake
Better watch out –
death and sleep
are the unknown

I want to sleep
comfortable, relaxed
awaking refreshed
That's my new mantra
not battling the old
but understanding
that gutteral fear –
loss, abandonment
out of control

Deep in my dreams
anything is possible
the monster might
rise from subconscious
and get me

Now that I know
there is no monster
just a frightened child
why do I still hide
from delicious sleep?

I 'm not the Little Diddle
youngest kid nomore
Now, as I become
more fully me
I can enjoy
contented rest

Just the thought of it
gives me the shakes
Deep dark death sleep
is a monster to hate

But what if it's not?
Maybe I should love it
If I loved my dreams
adrenaline fear
wouldn't rush me awake
as I neared sleep

All that wasted energy
turned into peaceful
recuperation
Yet that involves
trusting me enough
to believe I alone
can protect myself
from my mind's demon
that I created

What a long time coming
sewing up this tear

7 September 1999

MONDAY AFTER
OUR JOURNEY

Flying so high
with the light
bird of Bob,
freed from grief
self recrimination
on beach of peace

Magic Beach
turned right
Bob held –
transformed
after his journey
of broken arm

Everything
he touches
goes right

He is held
held in the heart
of my love stone
I gave to him

Me laughing
in water below,
watching him fly
joining with him

Soaring together
in clear blue
above Magic Beach

27 September 1999

BOHEMIAN HEAVEN

The shock of losing a friend.
Laboured breathing in hospital bed,
even smiling,
then lower lip ripe with emotion.
Wanting to live,
yet dying all the same.
Breathing, then a few hours later,
with Anne at your side,
leaving us behind
with mixed emotions.

David, you amazing paradox -
brilliant, but unable to stop drinking;
so self-centred,
yet deeply respectful of people;
a true rebel
in the heart of the establishment.

We'll miss you –
your coffee stained pictures
and wild poetry,
zest for life
in black leather jacket
with cigarette dangling from lip.
Speaking in foreign tongues
bringing cultures alive for us.

Those evenings round
your dining room table,
serving tangines and chocolate mousse,
the world dropping in to dine.
Discussions and song echoing out
your open window
to Trinity New Court below.
All your plans and schemes –
book projects, translations, poetry, art
your stamina, thrust for life
between hospital stays.

I'm glad I saw you again
in those last hours of breath.
There to know you better
to smile with you once again.
And now you leave us behind
as you journey into understanding.
And we try to do the same
enriched by your quirky, shining life.
May you find peace
in Bohemian heaven.

20 December 1999

My dear friend fear,
I bring an offering of peace,
so I may cushion you
in pink understanding,
resting back on comfy chair
gazing into warm fire.

From there I can see
you are made of my pain,
fear of being hurt again.
Churning that acidy poison
of my own imperfection.

With you at my side, dear fear,
the shortcomings of others are threats
and all I see are my own mistakes.

When I hold you
in a mother's arms
cradling my poor, hurt fear,
you slowly become
the child of love.

9 January 2000

Breathing from deeper place
not forced or controlled
just watched and felt.

Unwrapped from patterns,
binding so tightly,
I touch the calm
of soft, belly breathing;
a sanctuary beyond judgment.

Floating in sparkling cavern,
unhampered flow of breath,
layer on layer begins to unpeel
lightness of ease in my being.

Oh sweetness, may you stay with me often.

Dedicated to the Cambridge Sangha. A Sangha is a community that endeavours to practice the way of peace and awareness, together in harmony.

20 February 2000

A DAY OF MINDFULNESS

Coming together by bright coloured lantern
bringing food, anticipation, laughter,
exchanging news then slowly gathering
in living room turned shrine.

The sound of the bell
reminds me to breathe.
Bowing we acknowledge each other.
Sitting together, I settle on stool
built by my Sangha friend.
Thoughts flow by
as my body adjusts.
I witness a moment of torture,
surprised I allow it to pass.
But I want to dwell in love.
Yes, I feel it here with us.

Walking to the measure of my breath
in the circle of our concentration.
Our efforts building focus
in room alight with sunshine.

Sitting again I'm so grateful
touching this presence together.
Yum, this delicious moment
here for me to enjoy.
A fountain of white water
sprouts from the top of my head
cooling my body in its downward cascade.

With the bell the room reappears
and a time to sing the Heart Sutra,
a new version we've been practising,
plainsong rhythm, merging cultures,
echoing from the past.
Insight and sound in harmony
I shiver at the beauty of our union.

Lunch and merging culinary efforts
igniting succulent tastes.
In silence I remember
I don't need to eat more,
merely enjoy each mouthful.

The Dharma talk brings wisdom
that my pain is only impermanent.
As we share our listening and speaking
I see capacity of my Sangha friends
blooming through their living of Dharma.

Good humour abounds as we mingle
then gather for tea ceremony.
I watch in wonder at foreign traditions
taking deep root within.
Beyond external judgements
I'm pleased to just enjoy
the bowing, sipping of tea,
silent sharing of peace,
touching poetry essence.

As the room begins to darken
an atmosphere is apparent
a concentrated, timeless force
essential energy, alive with us,
flowing in harmony.

In hugging meditation
the tactile reminder
of our sacred intersection
together as never again
the coalescing of our Sangha.

After visiting my relatives in the United States

8 May 2000

Landing, after a weeks return,
settling into my space,
dwelling calmly within.
Pieces of self reunited
with glue of acceptance.

Befriending my spunky American,
touching the inner Jew,
holding uniqueness
beyond elitist fear.

Remembering, I enjoy
the pleasure of family,
the ease of old friends,
with a clearer state of mind.

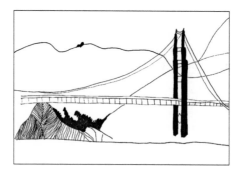

22 May 2000

In my begging bowl I see
what I fear is none other than me.
There, also, lies the possibility
to find only I can soothe my pain.
Only I can perform the miracle
to free myself from misperception
to look again and discover
that, in fact, the bowl contains
the blossom of my own acceptance.
All I need do to satisfy my craving
is feed myself with love.

LOVE IS ALL OPEN TO IT

In the slow presence
of sun and moon
stars and sky,
lying on warm sand
breathing in life's kiss,
I release my demons
of regrets and grudges.
In so doing
I forgive myself
freeing me to love anew.

In the buoyant sea of energy
place of my decendancy
I float in joyous serenity
beyond dragging weights
of my old despair.
Vistas open, I swim with fish
who fear not judgment,
untethered by sorrow's hook.

Later I see that fish hook
lodged around my breast bone.
Carefully I lift
and gently remove it,
understanding it may return
but I know the freeing way.

In dreams I spread my arms
rejoicing in peace.
Heart so open
I can see almond shaped
inner space.

In the stone circle,
in full presence
with the elements
I release bonds of fear
feeling my heart open
onto the earth,
sun's warm, healing touch.
Breathing in
sustaining waves of life,
hearing heaving tides.

Naked, I bath in the sea
washing away old deposits.
Dressing I prepare to start anew.
Leaving stone circle
I turn back to ask
how to be free
of recurring heartache.

The answer's so clear –
accept gifts of love.
It's that simple, accept gifts?
What a relief.
I can let myself do that.
It's far more pleasant
than loops of suffering.

I make my way back
on hilltop paths
overlooking sea and sky.
Smiling with my life partner,
contented hand in hand,
we move in transformation.

16 October 2000

ARE YOU SURE?

*After reading an excerpt from
Teachings on Love, by Thich
Nhat Hanh, I made an 'Are
you sure?' sign, which Thay
recommends to check
misperceptions.*

I lay down my plank
I use to beat myself
No longer needed
I see misperception
(habit of literal rigidity)
in fullness of forgiveness

Understanding obstacle
pillar of judgment
I thought I needed
to hold up my existence
I allow it to rest
on earth beside me

The wood disbands
as bud of acceptance
gradually emerges
Blossoming and blossoming
in groundswell of potential

I joyfully receive it
to flower in awareness
of non-attachment to views
Forgiveness countering guilt
Seeing I'm doing the best I can
in each moment of limited perception
Obscured most of all
by my pillar of judgment

A broader view emerges
in clarity of self-trust
Opening to my own gifts
I embrace myself
in clear light of love

6 November 2000

Accepting my anger
of college blockage
Touching that pain
with gentle awareness
compassion of knowing
how hard I tried

But conditions were unsuitable
for blooming women's courses
And I am too combative
though I try not to be
but to harness positivity for justice

In an atmosphere awash with negativity
I, too, am caught up and demoralized
So without blame, I release you, Joy
to use your energy in other directions

Perhaps looking back at this turning point
you'll be thankful it went this way
as the negative college whirlwind
seems too great to resist

Best to step away and look within
engage transformation potential
Accepting flaws and strengths
knowing great awakening is possible

To that goal I shift my energy
touching my open sores
with the balm of compassion
beyond judgment into poetry

11 December 2000

FAITH IN MAKING MONEY

Growing up, struggling for justice,
seeing 'money as the root of all evil'
having an aversion to creating wealth
feeling it would taint me,
destroy me with guilt,
expose my inner evil.

Now I don't believe in evil
only unskillful negativity,
misperceptions from fear
multiplied through generations
longing for release,
awaiting transformation
in the cycles of eternity,
from which perspective
they are but potential for love.

My desire for justice rejuvenated,
seeing it with greater clarity,
accepting purpose in making money
neither caught up in greed,
nor fearing its poison
keeping perspective –
a desire to live fairly
in unequal world,
to survive beyond desperation
having faith that cash will flow
through well-meaning energy.

Success, another great fear,
its inequitable nature –
bestowing such power
in profit society.

But I wish success to all,
not dependent on others' failure,
beyond oppressive roles
into earth's regeneration
where we are all
but momentary specks
in universe unbound.

26 December 2000

Take this day,
bare tree against foggy sky,
and see in it
the sun-lit spring of love.

In that vision
your trust will bloom,
allowing such possibilities
as you can not now conceive.

27 January 2001

HOLOCAUST REMEMBRANCE DAY

Waking in the night
to familiar mixture
of worry and dread
I suddenly recognize
this habit which seems
to predate my existence.
Out comes the word –
GRASPING.

I feel that clinging
squeezing my bowels
for illusive safety
from horror of pogroms,
refugee insecurity,
Holocaust remembrance.
Finding, again,
fear of 'deviant' Jew.

Hearing Thay's message
of love, understanding.
Power of compassion
shows me release,
as deep in belly
channels open,
beyond 'bad girl'.

Offering comfort for 'failings'
nurturing my sorrows
so I no longer need
to scheme to control
the changeable future.

Even Mom changed advice
she gave us as girls,
that women get things subtly,
manipulating behind scenes
as they lack the power
to openly confront men.

Now I see her point
avoiding confrontation,
while learning other ways
to just reconciliation.

In peace that follows
release grasping fear,
I commemorate Holocaust
in spirit of starting fresh
reusing suffering
to restore unbounded
life of the heart.

12 March 2001

BREATHING FOR JOY

In that sacred space
before going round
the hard time cycle
awareness to breathe
in very instant
where I abandon
my trauma for joy

In ocean of change
tiny fish enjoy sea
flowing with waves
high and low tides
in splendour of life
Gills taking in air
swimming through cycles
with ease of existence
reflecting blue sky

Preparing to go, with my whole family, to Plum Village,
the monastery and retreat centre of Thich Nhat Hanh

20 March 2001

JOY FOR PLUM VILLAGE

Experiencing such joy
sharing my practice
of breathing peace
with those I love
Oh what potential
to share the sanctuary
of Plum Village together

*I wrote this poem after taking the first Level of Reiki
training from Liz Barr. Reiki is a form of natural healing
and a spiritual practice with its origins in Japanese
Buddhism.*

10 June 2001

JUST FOR TODAY, TRUST

Reiki energy
added to aura
healing symbols
into psychic flow

Amazed to find
Reiki vibrations
really help
self and others

Life force energy
further focused
concentration
for deep release

Letting go of past
no judgment left
lessons learnt
struggles released

Gas and sweat
float up to clouds
pouring down
refreshing rain

Mending tears
in auric fields
building safety
in self/others

Grounded to earth
light through crown
restoring belly
vibrating palms

Healing energy
out through hands
joyous bliss
in joint communion

The ripples of my Reiki 1 attunement continue. An attunement allows a person to reconnect to the natural, healing energies of Reiki.

1 July 2001

Pregnant with life force
filling my cavity
spreading energy
setting intensions
to benefit all
with special focus
on my loved ones

Opening to them
this healing light
reversing the process
of worry and fear
releasing negativity
to positive intent

Body aglow
with light energy
Reiki, meditation
working together
helping me become
a being of acceptance
opening/transmitting
to self and others

15 August 2001

Sitting in garden warmth
content to be home
seeing my life anew
What a lucky person's
shoes I come to fill

Garden near river
Loving Family
Good Friends
Wonderful Sangha
Good Health
to cycle on through
And growing peace
deep in my heart

Life presents problems
that's part of practice
growing through change
accepting and being
In just this moment
the cool wind blows
helping me enjoy
a safe summer's day

Safe in myself
accepting dead tree
and wild nettles
Loving the garden
just as it is

8 September 2001

SAILING THE MIND

Silently gliding
through smooth waters
reeds rustling on shore
wind stirring leaves
and, oh, the thrill of life.

The wind picks up –
hold that rudder
grip that sail
gently, gently breathe.

In sudden gusts
sway starboard, port –
brace your feet
hold that sheet
shift through high and low.

Abrupt breach into reeds,
caught in swirling force –
the bump is nothing
so long as we
sail through our fear.

Lying on deck
rushing through Broad
childhood laugh and yelp,
with blue below and above
we are water and sky.

Oncoming boats
may well obstruct
not following 'right of way'.
But we hold our course
focusing on now
working out path as it comes.

In dreams I glide
on air current
above waves
wings spread
heart open.

Following September 11th destruction and fears of war to follow, the Sangha had a Day of Mindfulness. We read Thay's poem Call Me By My True Names, followed by mindful listening and speaking.

17 September 2001

We have been sitting
round this fire
of peace energy
for thousands of years.
This precious force
has warmed us
in coldest of winter.

Now as prospects seem bleak
peace is with us as we speak
of our suffering for those lost,
our fear for war ahead,
insights into causes,
compassion for all.

As the fire crackles
turning wood bright red
I see the timeless dream –
the hope of millions
that we can transform;
moving beyond reaction
toward the power of peace.

As we seek a loving response
to fear, hatred, injustice
what a special chance
to bring safety to all –
nurturing starving children,
embracing dispossessed,
respecting all peoples.

And in our own generosity
we create the safety we seek,
realizing this world is one
and fairness saves us all.

23 September 2001

HANDING OUT PEACE

Nurturing inner trust
holding fear/conflict
embracing my faults
soothing myself,
as the only way
to work for peace
out in the world.

On the pavement
at Campeace vigil
hundreds of people
signing petitions
yearning for an end
to cycles of conflict.

They, too, see
such spirals of hate,
fear unbounded
spinning back round –
terror in American
begetting further death
fuelling the hatred
for yet more terror.

Seeing and accepting
my own hate ways
causing such pain –
punishment habits
blaming myself
for other's sufferings
picking imperfections
with sharp tools of fear.

So there I stand
an American Jew
handing out leaflets
exposing wrongdoings
of America, Israel
grounded in love
of heritage and self.
Accepting us all
not as villains
but peoples of fear.

Now I'm also British
writing Prime Minister
pointing to hate spirals
asking his support
for way of forgiveness
finding justice through peace.

Thousands of miles away
my sister holds a sign
at her own vigil –
'Justice through peace'.
She tells me that beyond
our distant separation
we are together.
And I feel our bond,
from Mother serenity.

I also feel the link
with Muslim friends
working for peace
as we sit together
in interfaith unity
hearing our traditions
all seeking such peace.

And in that service
I find reconciliation
from Christian Minister
saying Paul would be horrified
at Christian wrongdoings
toward Muslims and Jews.
I accept his apology
as I set aside
Grandpa's hatred
for Russian Church
who taught the boys
that Jews killed Christ,
building their hatred
for terrible Pogroms.

As I forgive
those who transgressed
against my people,
I forgive myself
my own transgressions –
opening to the way
beyond cycles of blame.

Releasing myself
once again I begin
to release others,
holding my anger
in tender embrace
allowing me to stand,
imperfect as I am,
on the pavement
handing out peace.

11 October 2001

Working with fear
deep in solar plexus
holding that clay
soothing it gently
warming cold earth
through Reiki palms.

Tenderly kneading clay
making it supple
befriending dread
carried so long
I took it for granted.
Waking each morning
to burden of despair
heavy against the day.

Using any excuse
to reinforce blame –
grasping for judgment
conditioned response
life long habit
of finding the worst,
hoarding it there
deep in solar plexus.

Now what a relief
to have finally noticed
this physical point,
allowing me to focus
patient acceptance
on my own vital chakra.

Breathing in
out through you,
knowing I can stay.
No need to distract
to run with thoughts.
I have mindful anchor.

Preparing red clay
for my own creation,
spun on love wheel
into vessel of beauty
where I can breath deeply
opening to Joy of peace.

15 October 2001

SISTER ANNABEL'S RETREAT

Sister Annabel growing in me
reborn in us all at the retreat –
her radiant smile,
one pointed focus,
humility in imperfection,
joy in laughter.

Now savouring the remains
of that special time –
together when she announced
the start of bombing
calming our fears,
building Sangha strength.

My heart opening;
beyond worries
of war, disaster,
violence brought home,
to remember the need
to still my cycles
of negative growth;
focusing, instead, on nature –
waves and sea as one
foam blanketing pebbles
as we each stand together
being the water through time.

The silence so silky
soothing my heart
releasing judgment
into soft rose petals.

Stroking dog,
in warmth of sun,
lying on her back
accepting my touch
as mutual contentment.

Oh, such comfort, such comfort
holding Rahelly's hand
as we walk through space
grounded in each step
reborn in one another.

Aspiring to take the bodhisattva commitment
to enlightening myself and others so that all
beings may be liberated from suffering

12 November 2001

Seeking support from ancestors
contacting their line within me
feeling their strength to grow
here in this special moment.

Mother and mothers of mothers
back to great nature Goddess
nurturing, protecting, sustaining
so I may bloom from strong roots.

Fathers of Jewish tradition
keeping my peoples together
holding the spirit of faith –
tradition my cultural gift,
heritage rooting identity.

Spiritual exploration my anchor
breathing Buddha, Dharma, Sangha
allowing shifting perceptions
beyond conditioned response
into realization of harmony.

May all my roots support me
as I venture forth beyond trying
into bodhisattva existence
exploring inconceivable realms
grounded in ancestral wisdom.

I'm so glad to take you with me
all my spirit helpers on the path
so I may find my own way
toward Pure Land of peace.

May all my composted suffering,
nurturing black earth upon me,
nourish my energy of growth
building on ancestral roots
so I may flower as Joy anew.

This is really scary!

28 January 2002

Universe, humanity as one
a part of this wondrous whole
blessed in this very life
with tools and space to heal
able to grow beyond worries
seeing them as they are
sacred cycles of love
pointing the way to awareness.

Deep fear bubbles up
surfacing as stomach gas
long seeking release
leaving in its wake
a trail of acid
bringing to light
countless possibilities
of purity and vision
beyond mistakes
into concentration
where stability is possible
even as the wind
ravages all about.

Like mother tree
my roots go deep
to earth's solidity
where my trunk
breathes through gale
firm beyond fear
while branches sway.

And here I sit
rejoicing in acid
no longer afraid
of stomach pain.

Sipping spearmint,
breathing in wonder
in clarity, power
of Reiki energy
allowing my fears
to meander past.

In wind storm like this
clearing the air
for sun to shine.

10 February 2002

Touching old panic
of childhood fear –
kept back in school
laughed at by kids
as I stand alone
trying to read
symbols so strange.

Compensating madly
scurrying to keep up –
wild spellings block
my mind with fear.
Deeply held secret
which even today,
as author and teacher,
I rarely disclose.

Opportunity arising
after 30 year absence
to again be a student
on a different plane.

On my own terms
embracing my fear,
insight into origins
releasing the pain,
soothing the panic
of Sunday evenings
with homework undone
and mounting dread –
then rushing to finish
what I never understood
exactly how to start.

Now I teach others
secrets of structure
I need for myself.

Believing in them
as I can in me.
Revisiting old habits
long buried in blame
releasing that energy
to be reused again.

Building my confidence
stoking my fire
allowing myself
to be a 'learner'.

Suddenly teacher
is not enough
sacred student
is also my role.
Beyond dirty image
of streaming so low,
in class position
of common girl role
into deep blooming
of confidence anew.

Trusting my vision,
dyslexic as it is,
finding within it
that creative space
to use connections –
strange as they seem –
to revisit dread,
school intimidation,
academic failure,
to gain the insight
for myself and others
to support us all
in learning to learn.

After connecting with the Reiki
Distant Healing Symbol

11 February 2002

Distant Healing
Ultimate Dimension
crossing time/space
in Einsteinian reality –
glimpse of existence
as more than this plane.

Feeling the force
being in fingers
everywhere/nowhere
just part of all.

This smallest glimpse
allowed by trust
I muster this moment,
releasing my fear
of unknown future.
Seeing past planets,
stars, galaxies
to moment of typing
here and now.

Everywhere/nowhere
interconnected
in plane of reality
so rich and sweet.
I dare not enter
feeling unworthy.

Dimensional spread
out beyond and back –
comes that intension
to be who I am
allowing life flow
in river that's me
from stream to sea
and back all at once.

3 June 2002

DAD'S TRANSFORMATION

Deep, deep beyond distraction
lies a space of open wings
There I sit, expanding
Present through storm and calm
watching, being, breathing

It's hard to witness
Dad's transformation
from life to death –
process of returning
to family essence

I want to hold
the Dad I knew –
in control
strong and sure

Yet I find such beauty
in what Dad's become –
accepting recipient
of family support
expressing such love
gratitude, approval

We're sure in our love all round
which makes this process strong
Pure beauty in unity connected
Mom's legacy beyond time/space
supports as we witness the change
which time will bring to us all

And in that process
I touch my fear
with gentle understanding,
reassuring that scared little girl
that her parents will always be there
It's merely the form that changes
not their kernel of love
which as a family we share

26 August 2002

RED MOON RISING

Waking from dreams of fear
into morning sunlight
rising to healing vibrations
trusting heart to open

Sitting in meditation
accepting universal love
beyond cycles of pain
where hate waves overtook

Viewing back into time
ready now to release
with Reiki past healing
Seeing the inner hook
Removing power connection
Allowing wound to settle

Dwelling in safety of love
allowing me to become
the healing force I am
shining within/without

May I spread life force love
as a part of all beings
touching that inner smile
accepting pain, imperfection
trusting the light of healing
to glow forth within me
to become a shining healer

In this process may I become
the very force I seek
Back round in this life
to being the rustling wind
joy of sea blue immersion
pink of sky with red moon rising

1 September 2002

Goddess of Compassion
flowing through centuries.
Ancestral underground
bubbling up to me.

Coming to old symbols
resonating anew.
Vibrations being passed
through energy stream.

Reverberating in me,
child of Florence
Jewish seeker
descendent wanderer.

Searching for way to peace
listening for sound of bell
hearing deep resonation
striking past connection.

Compassion Goddess Priestess
healer of self and beyond
watching the way within
spreading peace without.

Gaining strength of trust
allowing energy through
past fearful blocks
to be perfectly good.

Beyond trying too hard
golden safety shines
if I just succumb
allowing trust to guide.

My sacred imperfection
this human form endows
is perfect exploration
of suffering/joy as one.

If I let momentum
flow into future
I find healing teacher
I was seeking all along
is smiling through my lips
flowing through my hands
shining from my heart.

Oy, Ga – vol – t!
I'm scaring myself good,
laughing myself silly
Oy, yoy yoy, yoy yoy!

3 September 2002

Writing for digestion
blending insights
converting fear
collecting dispersion
into nourishing soup

16 September 2002

Wiping mud off windscreen
allowing sunlight through
freshening way
for trip beyond expectations
to places unimaginable
where beauty unfolds
through mulch of suffering

23 September 2002

Reiki Moon Haiku

Full moon in third eye
white iris heals dread, opens beam
divine light joins all

After reading David Brazer's Zen Therapy, I saw that my own life's difficulties were the most useful koan. A koan is a puzzle which cannot be solved by logic and concepts, but only through insight.

24 September 2002

Trust the light
beyond koan knot –
impossible contradiction
to fathomable paradox –
when seen from far

Life's Koan hard
to take and swallow
but bitter pill
just way of growing
through riddle ring
into glow beyond

Things have a way
of working out,
when you surrender
to positive trust
beyond worry loop
into realm
of life force delight

I hold my fear
in tender embrace
allowing the venom
of poisonous blame
to drain away
change once again
back into growth

From there I see
I can only do
my own riddle
I trust loved-one
to find her way
through her own

After doing the third level of Reiki
and having an attunement

23 October 2002

Trust life force flow
working its own way
through my channels
to my essence
filling belly pool

Holding breath of faith
in this very instant
love is content
allowing power stream

Exhaling control
letting judgement go
Healing energy
through Reiki symbol
bursts into joy

What a blessing
believed impossible
childhood dream
to be a healer!

My body aligned so that I no longer
needed the lift in my shoe, which I'd
worn for years for my shorter leg, after
I became a Reiki Master Teacher. A
Reiki Master is able to attune other
people to the healing energies of Reiki.

29 October 2002

Balancing back
equanimity flow
through fear's grasp
to secret guilt
centuries stored

Releasing slowly
as I ripen
mellowing into
Reiki love

May this energy
cleanse my being
allowing radiance
out to others
healing light
of nurturing justice

After anti-Semitic barb, while giving out peace leaflets

10 November 2002

This gift of peace
allowing protection
so even my deep fear
of Jew hating toward me
can bring me love not anger

Tenderly nursing my wound
smoothing my broken aura
soothing jagged alarm
returning to natural state

Disempowering effect
of bearer of hate
allowing me protection
greater than negative spin

In that changing process
releasing gripping fear
which can resurrect
hurt/pain again

I open my hands
from prayer of peace
rebuilding trust anew
shining harmony
out to those
who would hate me

May they feel lighting of love
thunderbolt of compassion
breaking through fear
reversing negative spin
allowing diversity accord

2 December 2002

Dear life partner
I send to you
my deep respect
for creating a way
to begin the process
of healing the past
to be a family again

Dear life partner
I send to you
my deep esteem
for your way
to bypass blame
into fresh clearing
where sacred healing
can be nurtured

Dear life partner
I send to you
my special thanks
for being my friend
through rocky times
and smooth as well

Dear life partner
I send to you
this blooming rose
red and fresh
as our love
strong and secure

Dear life partner
I trust your power
into the realm
of creative endeavour
where you are strong
when open to faith
in your own muse

Dear life partner
in your adventure
in touching the past
your special place
of earthly being
from youth forest
returns its wonder
with richness of wisdom

Dear life partner
I send to you
my open love
for our journey
down life's river
together

8 December 2002

Bare tree on grey sky
Candle sparkles light through
Mantle passed to me

10 December 2002

On bird's wing
beyond thought's grasp
soars open space

From nature's flow
beyond nagging doubt
runs easy stream

From easy stance
beyond body tension
comes soft release

In bird song
beyond hoarse fear
sounds love's melody

In no future
beyond plan's grasp
is now energy

In this now
beyond any care
peace resonates

25 January 2003

There upon the green
stood a great, tall tree
Scottish variety transplanted
into rich soil of Fen.

Together with his partner,
strong Canadian mix,
they blossomed, matured,
weathered storms
grew in love's beauty
and birthed from this union
two wondrous saplings.

Over the years Great Tree
spread his vision through Fens
collecting films afar
playing them here for us.
With his special humour
gentle brand of kindness
twinkle of eye, sharpness of mind
he brought his insights and art.

In the warmth of meals
cooked in wondrous style
served with affectionate delight,
much talk and good wine;
we came to mingle minds
mulling film, politics, life
seeing scenarios of gloom
as well as friendship of light.

Deep in winter's darkness
came a powerful storm
there on flatness of Fen
Great Tree was caught in whirlwind
swept up in its fierce might.

Sudden force of gale
took down our Great Tree
toppling him root and all.

In the stillness that followed
oh, such sadness and shock
to find Great Tree, so loved,
was taken beyond life.
Distant sound of church bells
chiming deep connections
there between all times
here in rays of sunlight
breaking through the darkness
shining upon his trunk
fallen yet in attendance
here within us all.

In the dawn that follows
such unthinkable tragedy
the earth opens up her heart
the sun shines upon
strong partner and saplings
held within our warmth
sheltered by our love
as we come together
in this time of mourning.

Nature's organic process
recycles Great Tree's wood
embraces his life force energy
reabsorbing it into universe.

May we find the vision
to see beyond disaster
growing beyond our sorrow
helped by Great Tree's love
and our support surround
into lightness of spring
and the beauty of summer.

Preparing for my upcoming ordination into the Core Community of the Order of Interbeing. The Order of Interbeing was established by Thich Nhat Hanh during the Vietnam War with a commitment to the principles of Socially Engaged Buddhism.

3 February 2003

Recognising sand castles
built in the air
seeing delusion
constructed false security
habitual comfort
in scheming plans

Realising clearly
that I drifted away
smiling at joke
of sandcastles in air
laughing out loud
at root of my fear

Not laughing at you
dear Mommy longing child
but laughing with you
Us dripping wet sand
as Mom shows us how

I know you are here
sweet mother of mine
smiling in imperfection
radiating love
engaged in my backbone's
releasing of fear

Beyond complications
of photos and details
lies the essence
of our family love

May you be with me
dear mother of mine
when I touch the earth
in deep ordination
harmonising with Quan Yin
into Interbeing Order

All my ancestors,
friends, bodhisattvas
come join me as well
as we smile to life

Sister Jina, the Abbess of Lower Hamlet, transmitted the 14 Mindfulness Trainings to me in Plum Village. The 14 Mindfulness Trainings are the precepts of the Order of Interbeing, written by Thich Nhat Hanh.

02 March 2003

TAKING THE 14 MINDFULNESS TRAININGS

Pink dawn spreads awakening
over dark sky with crescent moon
In lotus pond in winter respite
life reflects coming of light

I stand alone/together
being broadening sight
opening arms, soaring
touching other dimension

Awakening latent insight
forgetting all my fear
allowing me to be, once again,
the very spirit of birth

Touching earth in ceremony concluded
sisters and brothers breathing with me
witnessing/being on our path

Taking trainings of shining way
touching earth as Mommy is here
receiving safe-heart of Sister Jina
opening my being to life anew

Wordless words I move beyond
releasing conceptions, prisons built high
allowing flow to take me up
swaying in childhood freedom
laughing and playing
dancing with the wind

Yesterday's peace march celebrating Mom's
birthday through transformation

Sunday, 23 March 2003

In heavy wartime
when depression lurks
I hold awareness
as life's protection
from predawn spin
into depths of despair
where Iraqi suffering
burns out of control
and I am helpless

Better to remain
in life force glow
sending love
to those who suffer

Energy of thousands
marching though London
force for peace
power reborn
in new generation

This moment of war
is awakening path
as we walk together
I breathe and tread
pavement in boots
worn to touch
Plum Village peace

After a deep meditation together on
my first Order of Interbeing Retreat

13 April 2003

Back to childhood sense
remembering connections
natural as breathing
to help all people
wishing them well

Belly reconnection
there all the time
awaiting my release
from fear tangles
to touch sameness

Being on that train
momentum of awareness
still long journey
yet I've arrived
in this moment

Connected on-route
commitment made
direction chosen
relaxed on TGV
warm safe journey
with Avalokita

Seeing my first grandchild, Sophie, with her
parents in hospital, the day after her birth

24 April 2003

Touching newborn
granddaughter's hand
touching the universe
back through time
touching Mom
reborn in her
as she falls asleep
in my arms
into deep peace
of Mom's serenity

Sophie's first visit, with her parents, to our home

3 May 2003

Gleaming Sophie comes to us
a being of her own, Mom's shared delight
Adding to family, changing dynamic
bringing together blocked well-meaning
shifting roles, radiating inclusion
opening our hearts to cosmic love

This warm, blessed baby links
my heart to her in tender innocence
connecting relatives, near and far
including 'machetunim'
stretching from Wales
to Holland, Eritrea
as we become a Cambridge family

24 May 2003

Tending my flame
koan remembered –
old loved-one's spin
with insight vision
lighting beyond

What pain again
here in my heart
cracked with sorrow
suffering cold blast
circling back round

Feeling my flame
needing protection
surrounding glow
with solid stones
sheltering my fire
from gusts of wind

With that heat
energy, power
embracing my sorrow
Safe in life flame
sheltered there
I sigh out relief

Steady, steady
as deep winds blow
touching strength
to see beyond

Opening my heart
to feel the pain
plus loving trust
that allows for shift

Witnessing power
of transformation
beyond just me
interweaving beauty
of energy love

To these lessons
of pain I open
to learn and return
to pink glow of light
within and beyond
protecting, expanding
past veil of life's play

29 June 2003

HERB GARDEN GROWTH

Reiki, heart talk and weeding
washed down with lots of water
manifestation preparation
balancing earth and sun

After years of planning
turning over the soil
allowing change to happen
with Sangha friend's support

Beyond separation from earth
discomfort with her plants
lies my deep fascination
desire for connection to life

Feeling thick earth clay
remembering childhood time
Mom's allowance to eat dirt
in tiny square under tree

Imaging plan for space
trusting Simon's knowledge
Him taking me into process
moving, arranging, shifting

Digging in the plants
I touch the roots of growth
caught in circular motion
awaiting room on my plot

Herb garden emerging
amazing and thrilling
transformation of space
beyond my ability alone

Planting big centre piece
Bay Tree to keep as bush
I smile at cooking flavour
tired yet satisfied

I look and look again
at unity and diversity
Can herb garden be here
right outside my door?

Exhausted I take to bed
where nibbling doubts emerge
too much space for weeds
should have shifted dill

Now I smile and laugh
with silly friend old pattern
releasing control illusion
allowing life to flow

Whatever happens to plants
the way of process grows
savouring magic essence
of life in my garden

23 August 2003

Speaking to Dad
happy and joking
our laughter mingling
in interconnection.

Roosevelt, he says,
had compassion for all.
What a wondrous world, we agree,
if everyone did the same.

'Mishpocheh' far and wide –
all people 'mishpocheh', I suggest.
Thinking Dad agrees,
if you count back to monkeys.

Joking Dad goes on
about ancestor monkey Joe.
So deep and wide his laugh.
So happy to laugh together.

24 August 2003

SUSPENDING DISBELIEF

Floating up high
above tangles
clinging to feet
engulfing blame

Seeing more clearly
enmeshing net
even when
I am caught

In this process
of disentanglement
many recurrences
some glimpses of joy

Joyous connections
draw me up
in energy love
beyond control need

Judgement
old habit
is but a thread
able to tear

But do come in
old habit of mine
how bored you must be
how twisted and sore

Enmeshed as you are
in fear and projection
how happy us both
to float up to freedom

From there I can see
the joys of peace
the tangles of loved ones
that pain me so

Releasing for me
what better way
to understand them
in joyful connection

Cutting teaching to half time, able to attend
weekly Sangha meditation

4 September 2003

Celebration of new beginnings
joining weekly meditation
with Sangha at healers' home
settling deep into calm

Shifting into new stride
beyond 'need' to do
into current of being
allowing life to happen

Combining into one person
bringing together my parts
disparate avenues merging
returning to whole of me

Reiki my healing essence
ready for wider role
accepting fear beyond panic
trusting positive force

Interbeing with Sangha
becoming Order Member
Mystery name yet to come
allowing possibilities to flow

Releasing tangles of loved-one
enjoying family as is
Savouring deep blessings
that Bob and Kev bestow

College, my dear sustenance
Luck for .5 in two days
No need for anger rut
when this is an opening

Connecting with students, staff
allowing help to flow
practicing detachment
with growing awareness

What fortune in the sunshine
in good health I walk the green
seeing insects and grasses
hearing leaves chime in wind

12 September 2003

Hearing morning dread
'Oh, not another day'
I'm pleased to have surface
old chorus of distain
in which I can find
kernel of draining
energy leak
tear in my aura

Origin exploring –
bad girl, dirty Jew
school children laughing
at how I can't read
Fear of no plan
nothing to do
scattering me open
to face myself

There I find
scared little girl
scratched and beset
with deep disapproval

To her I bring
arms open wide
her real protection
is my awareness

What do I feed
unconscious habit
sucking my energy
for so many years?

There before me
is self disgust
Such a dark secret
must be suppressed

But hurt little girl
needs my attention
I hold my heart
to feed her with love

It's alright dear heart
I know you are paining
bad girl/bad mother
spinning back round

I breathe, accept you
restoring life of heart
accepting, accepting
deep scar still unhealed

With Reiki heat
left side focus
energy flows
into scared being

There taken in
soothing depression
renovating balm
bringing such ease

Warmth pours through
to negative flow
reaching cycle of scold
where I smile you with love

Suddenly I laugh
this isn't just a poem
taking child's hand
together we dance

Gurgling growls
pour from my mouth
baby sounds
surfacing anew

Attention, attention
I give to my cry
I will attend you
dear heart of mine

The arrival of my Order of
Interbeing Ordination Certificate,
with my new Dharma Name of
True Wonderful Commitment,
which Thay had given me

8 October 2003

Unknown wonders
arriving by post
uncanny timing
message united –
commitment fruits

Ordination Certificate
vibrates depth
of Thay's energy
touching hands
back to Buddha

Shock at name
slowly finding
my courage
in accepting
commitment virtue

Here within
shining through
undervalued
viewed as donkey
feared as grasping

True Wonderful Commitment
This life's energy
viewed from perspective
shining new light
on quality within

Seeing inner rigidity
such fear grows
obscuring light
starry connection
all the way back

Seeing ancestors'
deep need to cling
missing, forgetting
their laughter, vision
for sweetness of life

My great guilt
blinkering vision
overshadowing
in heavy cloud
obscuring light

Commitment
discernment
vision to see
when to persist
when to release

Oh, sweet commitment
so hard to value
merit awaiting
my clear acceptance
of who I am

Florence's daughter
here clear and true
literal lineage
yet such jewel
in living heart

Then comes also
today in the post
Kevin's gift
Note so touching
for Bob and I

'To my parents,
who won't give up
on the dream...
thank you,
your son, Kevin'

I take refuge
in that dream
of just peace
and that dream
takes refuge in me

7 November 2003

Breathing in
wind swept leaves
Inner self
golden universe
feeling link

May I keep connection
beyond distracting webs
anger visited upon me
Still remaining present
perspective, understanding

Growing through process
turmoil to peace
glimpsing clearer vision
smiling out to life
breathing every step

Hugging with Bob
cuddling lives together
basking in his love
shining mine upon him
being in our presence

3 December 2003

Intension to freshen
open to light
feeling soft glow
pink and purple
where hurt surfaces

Contagious despair
negative spin
consuming me
when I lose
my awareness

In time of trouble
what great need
for Mom's serenity
Thay's clarity
Reiki's light

All qualities
growing within
there on call
when I return
to breath root

When I lose it
that's also life
seeing, accepting
returning again
to concentration

I woke in the night to write down this poem,
soon after Dad died.

4 January 2004

Dad, we went down to the sea
oxygen, you and me
The shoreline expanse
the seagull sky dance
your eyes gleaming, breathlessly

Your energy still intent
With walker you slowly persist
in going out to eat
Singing on to the last
Participating in life

Holding hands, eyes connect
Together we drink in the view
If only Mom could see -
So now, Dad,
with her you can be

Taking my time to accept
you merging with sea expanse
As waves break into mist
and water just changes form
So energy you become

The beauty of that vista
where sea and sky touch
Along that horizon plane
there our eyes still meet
with Mom, through generations

As Susan and I carry on
the family within us now
Grandchildren and beyond
your legacy stretches on
the full length of the shore

15 January 2004

I.

Allowing myself
to slip back
into mourning Dad

Walking in cold
holding his hand
in step across time
Mom joins, other side

Between bouts of loved-one
in nervous breakdown mode
me switching into calm
focused awareness
Still her panic energy
sucks at my heart

I release control
just do what I can
still jet-lagged, shaken
but hearing birds call

Coming back
to Reiki meditation
connecting to source
In through crown
spread through body
out through skin
returning to source

Tears come and go
I feel Dad, Mom support
I want to be there for Dad
but I'm so drained
Still I send my love
in his time of transition
learning to be alone
while so much apart
of universe, Mom, us

II.

On earth plane
as I practice
with Life Koan
I work to retain
build, fortify
mindful awareness
clear protection
touching detachment
trusting universe

All I can do
is enjoy blue bird
passing cloud
sadness and love

31 January 2004

Oh, finality of loss
on physical plane
brought by death

No more Dad to touch
speak to on the phone
sing old songs together

Now his Yiddish
rests with me
fleeting as it is

Passage of time
end of generation
in Magezis line

Yet I do still feel
you are here with me
on the spirit plane

As water flows down
so senior generation
I do become

Such sadness I touch
while such bright eyes
you smile out intently

Photographs a link
my head on your shoulder
your hand on mine

Walking along the shore
between visits to Mom
in her earlier death process

The family is back together
you told her in intensive care
her eagerly awaiting my visit

Looking beyond judgement
guilt and despair
accepting separation pain

Oh, dear process of mine
dear transformation for Dad
may we support each other

28 February 2004

Psychic surgery
for self hatred
taken back into
past life view

There killed
by knife
to heart
on my side

Such old pain
vaguely remembered
brought to contact
for relief now

Don't want it anymore
Don't need it, let it go
time to release
it's enough, enough

I forgive
the stabber
I forgive myself
I forgive myself

Oh such deep habit
genetic guilt to heal
illusion of control
illusion of power

I can't change loved-one
though mother role prescribes
I take on her life
I must save myself

Taking on her pain
is more than I can bare
nether does it help
but to hurt us both

Doctor says I'll die
if I don't set limits
She needs limits too
for that I must trust

Oh I want to trust
to cut the gold cord
needing to be needed
Self sustenance first

Psychic surgery
on myself
this morning
cutting out old way

Bruised and confused
by energy drain
taking on pain
agreeing to assault

Working through
old wounds
Healing
does take time

Give myself the love
open to the light
let the process be
trust in life force

Accept worry happens
we take time to heal
in this big challenge
great potential lies

Reiki power symbol
I put in my chakras
May I be protected
safe enough to heal

May loved-one find
her own healing too
I release my need
to be in 'control'

I can choose illusion
or larger view
in past lives
many children too

Even many parents
as mine return to whole
I hold their hands
reconnect anew

Thank you for your love
wisdom passed to me
Dad, joy of life
Mom, serenity

25 March 2004

Albatross Jewel
may I use you
to shine on through

Beyond misperceptions
spring blossoms anew
I open toward light

Budding yet again
dark energy also present
I accept as part of life

In that acceptance
insight, understanding
distance, disconnection

Detachment from my fear
loved-one's binding hook
Future always unknown

In that clarity of vision
may I come of wisdom
living moment by moment

Seeing through helplessness
desperation grasp
giving up 'why me?'

There that place of sadness
this I do embrace
accepting life as is

Beauty also beckons
shining bird atop
bare tree budding spring

Flap wings into clouds
distant pink sunset
beauty/sadness one

Deep dimension perspective
beyond judgement/shame
shining jewelled reflection

Preparing to travel to Plum Village with my loved-one

1 May 2004

Faith connection to ultimate
release fear of failure
guilt washed away by rain

May Day of the spirit
connected to life's energy
light green balance of love

Smoke of tee tree oil
drifting back beyond
breathing into lungs

Seeing through third eye
Lower Hamlet clarity
childhood peace on swing

Embarking into unknown
preparing for spiritual journey
healing voyage with loved-one

Plum Village possibilities
for me to open up to healing
only loved-one can open herself

May Buddhas and bodhisattvas
be with her to find her way
to path of peace she seeks

Her journey's beyond my control
I can't know what's best for her
but I can be with life as it comes

May I enjoy this day
being with my grown children
awareness for safety and love

19 June 2004

RELEASING DESPAIR

It's OK
You've been through a lot
You need to recover
Be gentle with me
understanding

Release duty to others
help them by practicing
kindness to self
Calm – Smile
even to old ruts

Too much to describe
No need to retell
sadness, despair
wonder and light

Processing life
resolving, accepting
loved-one and self
I'm gutted yet whole
widening camera lens
to see summer beauty

A part of bigger picture
Sophie's big smile
laughing together
Bob and I talk
Parents here with me
serenity and zest

May I be peaceful
May I touch whole
there in wider vision
life in perspective
releasing despair

10 August 2004

Solar plexus yellow sun
shine within my being
of deep sadness and joy
anointed with balm of love

Just for today my dear
I shall take care of you
looking from the inside
seeing with eyes of love

From there so very clear
anger for self protection
ineffective backfires
keeping middle hollow

Looking out for me
beyond wrestling match
releasing inner hooks
detachment to be free

Detach from guilt and shame
anger, aversion and fear
touch inner need
so self caring grows

How can I care for others
with my own needs so great?
only example can help them
where I can save myself

Looking after me
feeling energy flow
beyond childhood loops
into great ocean of all

Against upbringing grain
love me for how I can be –
pleasing or defiant
reacting from outer place

Just for this day
I shall take care of you
seeing from fresh inner view
sunbeam piercing clouds

So simple starting from here
clearly mindfulness way
detaching from loved-one
emerging renewed Joy

Daddy I help us both
heal into our ownness
not there to please others
first we must love inner self

Touching our misgivings
self forgiveness, inner vision
seeing our own true needs
tender internal focus

From there vision is simple
what to do is clear
in this moment smile love
from deep inner care

No one out there to please
nothing out there to prove
inner meaning so easy
listen to that self

All I want is peace
regain composure lost
settle with clearer vision
that truly all is well

Easy from that perspective
to know what to do and not
glimpsing inner sun
to shine harmony out

12 November 2004

Beautiful reality
beyond mind catch
sad for her pain
past my control

River still ripples
with mirrored sky
trees upside down
leaves float by

Grass deep green
streaked with sun
leaves once yellow
now crunch brown

Green beaked duck
feathered bright
paddles on by
seeming to glide

All of us
have our own work
mine opening crown
to let in the light

20 January 2005

Moving beyond loved-one
Heartsick pain release
Allowing our lives to shift
giving her space to heal

My old friend worry
I give you room to change
Healing time is now
for me to grow and help

Treating Reiki clients
cleanses my own self
building my focus
Trusting the light

Vietnam, the wonder
of Thay returning home
Reconciliation smiles
Teaching, oh, so great

I'm given this gift
by Dad and Mom
Adventure, serenity
to follow my teacher home

So I release my fright
worry of preparation
Fear of being unworthy
fret of robe wrong size

Hair parting shift
allowing pain to pass
Trusting my inner focus
Returning to life force love

3 February 2005

I choose happiness, once again
Out of the depths of despair
came this longing for happiness
now opening as an orchid in heart

Across grey winter sky
birds fly and float
Touched by their song
I watch them glide

I watch worry mind
then feel peace presence
discovering once again
they both live within

I have a choice
here in this moment
In detached awareness
I choose pink heart

Again it comes back
as Mom used to say,
'It's all the way
you look at things'

Echoed by Phuong
mirrored in us
from depths of being
springs fountain of life

I still remember
how Phuong said
my aura was gold
there last Tet

My New York wish
to lighten heart with love
still resonating through
Hilda Shanty Davi

3 March 2005

HAPPY BIRTHDAY ME, MOM & DAD

Merry-go-round elation
mirroring childhood delight
allowing Joy to glow

Happy birthday, my friend
Returning to peace vibration
releasing terror of year

Trust slowly returns
shell-shocked
but deepened

All part of the way
No need to cling
now is time for joy

VIETNAM POETRY INTRODUCTION

for Buddhist Art Week Cambridge Library Exhibition

After thirty-nine years
my teacher, Thich Nhat Hanh
returned to Vietnam
bringing reconciliation

The wake of that energy
travelled far and wide
with thousands coming
to hear Thay speak

Listening they learnt
his Zen practice
to walk and live
in present moment

This awakened Monk
was exiled while abroad
speaking there for peace
during Vietnam War

Leaving as a single cell
of Vietnam Sangha whole
he grew International Sangha
returning with monastics and lay

I was blessed to be part
of healing delegation
all these years later
when the time was ripe

My poems here below
written during that trip
come out of mindful practice
meditation brought to life

During wondrous process
of inner/outer journey
met people who years before
I worried over during war

Admiration for
lives, land reconstructed
In teacher's shining light
I received gift of courage

7 May 2005 – Cambridge

On the way to Hanoi

18 March 2005 – Bangkok

Golden Buddha splendour
resonating with Thai Chants
I join in vibration
at home in foreign land

Suddenly in majority
of black haired Buddhists
I find deep peace
sitting on Temple floor

Bangkok towers sprawl
between dilapidated homes
Posh Air Con Malls
and Humid Market Stalls

Pollution blocks the sun
Skywalks above teeming masses
King powered nation
Skytrain speeds on

Such friendly smiles
We all bow with ease
Buddhist well wish
and Capitalist drive

River bustling artery
boat called by whistle
longtail, pirate, tour
express boat that stops

We jump on
crowded with mix
Monks, shoppers, tourists
Thai, foreign together

Lunch at water's edge
I can say 'not hot'
Anabel and I share
synchronicities in our lives

Bargaining at bazaar
Dad would be proud
Thai silk beauty
in parents' gift to me

22 March 2005 – Hanoi

Thay's talk today
to 'Vietnamese Abroad'
ambassadors, officials
scientists, business people

Acceptance, reconciliation
finding commonality
Monastics good Communists
no money or possessions

Paradise of Communism
available here and now
Already have ingredient
of mindful breath

Party organizer
asks Thay to pass word
Vietnam is open
The past is past

Monastic chanting
healing force
a privilege to be
a part of Viet peace

23 March 2005 – Hanoi

Hanoi bustle
Learnt to cross street
Focus and trust
walk slowly forward

Walking meditation
on Hanoi streets
silent solidity
in midst of buzz

Motor bikes zoom
everyone sells
food, fruits, all goods
we breathe by

Down to the lake
along the path
traffic zooms
water softly ripples

I choose the lake
green growth
Pagoda centre
being the beauty

24 March 2005 – Hanoi

To the temple
It's happening today
preparation replaced
by shock of reality

Temple gate beauty
shrine to sister
Sister gives talk
we join the Sangha

Gifts galore
temple robe
and bowl
ticket to Binh Dinh

Putting on the cloth
a part of the whole
mindful walking
silent eating

Return to Plum village
right here in Vietnam
Thay wants us here
to show lay practice

Sister says that
the government
is becoming
fond of us

I am fond
of being here
thrilled, excited
enjoying it really

26 March 2005 – Hanoi

In newspaper, TV
Thay meets Prime Minister
last night at big talk
young Vietnamese clap

Economic-Culture club
head praises Thay
as one of great
religious leaders

Message to professors
move beyond knowledge
Buddhist essence
touching happiness now

Devotional practice
of Northern temples
doesn't appeal
to youth seeking peace

Teaching breathe, smile
walking touching earth
awakening inner life
transforming anger

The night before
teaching in English
Thay repeats lesson
I hear of anger anew

Sitting close to front
feeling Thay's light
his smile radiating
his message fresh

Yes, I do need
to sign peace treaty
with the person
of myself

There in depths
darkness of muck
still unresolved
suffering of old

Exploration
in fine paper journal
tenderly holding
watching pain

Monastic chants
Accepting me
Mom's soothing
Release, transformation

Today back to temple
Plum Village joy
Dharma discussion
Pagoda, Buddhist flags

Vietnamese country scenes
rice paddies and lakes
French style homes
and muddy shacks

In rain and cold
unexpected weather
in farms and cities
people work so hard

Road construction
buildings go up
in fortune of peace
Vietnam smiles

28 March 2005 – Halong Bay

Gliding past small islands
stretching up from green water
with tree topped hair
at Halong Bay

What peace
steaming along
no sign of mines
long past

Atop hill
red pagoda
against grey sky
fog hovering at base

Cleansed, we're blessed
to see effect
of war turned to peace
friends' reconstruction

Yesterday Yen Tu Mount
crowds gathered for fest
climbing muddy rock steps
to Zen King's home

I climb with Nhu
74 year old pilgrim
Holding hands I support her
others come past and help

With grey robe, brown jacket
I'm less an outsider
Nhu translates comments
I laugh in Vietnamese

At hermitage in cliff
I manage quiet space
I hear, 'just be'
smoke rising from incense

Closing eyes I see island
like those we pass now
When at home in my island
inner temple will shine

At heart of island
there wondrous cave
stalactites drip beauty
into silent pond

Sangha walks through cave
Chants to Avalokita
Feeling old water energy
Releasing mind to joy

Cleansing energy wash through
allow suffering to pass
just as Halong Bay
returned to true beauty

Post Script

A walk on the beach
before returning to Hanoi
bus driver chooses place
mass tourist construction

30 March 2005 – The Road to Binh Dinh from Da Nang

Bus bumping
Springs squeaking
Journey on through
endless rice fields

Sleepy from 4:30 start
Dreamy through passing towns
Road lined with small shops
Front rooms selling same goods

We travel on south
Green rice turns yellow
Harvesting happens
Cone hats, bent backs, sickles

Near My Lai Massacre
Fields now green with growth
Such suffering and death
recycled by land, people

People work so hard
Fruits of labour shine through
In patchwork quilt fields
neighbours work together

Haystacks piled high
made of rice stalks here
Flags out for their fest
Thirty year war victory

Now we near the sea
beyond salt fields
Sister tells of old home
White waves, clear sand

Off the bus we go
Onto peace-time beach
Old bunker behind
Young monks jump in sea

Others joyfully follow
Soon half the Sangha's wet
Brown robes in blue sea
Laughter fills the air

What landings has Sahuvn seen?
Now death destruction behind
The beach beckons wide
We laugh and smile with life

31 March 2005 – Binh Dinh Province Temples

Rice Paddies
Stalk stacks
Cone hatted peasants
cut rice by hand

On roads, front gardens
rice spread out to dry
Each patch of earth farmed
green in time of peace

To rural temple we go
Beyond fishing boats at sea
After splendor of mass temple
country one is small, simple

After procession, ceremony
Women feed us lunch
But as we're so many
I eat in overspill

In shade of mid-day heat
women watch us eat
'You Like?' I nod and smile
trying my meager Viet

Old women so tiny
watch and seem pleased
We giant foreign sisters
enjoy eating their food

Like sweet potato
tasting of chestnut
cooked on open fire
I smile, offer thanks

She comes and sits beside me
sweetly holding my hand
Smiling through blackened teeth
A few words go so far

'Anh', Yes from England
Her beauty shines through
May I take your picture?
Digital, so you can see

Kids suddenly appear
laughing to see photos
So we take more
Then giggle at pics

In openness of country simplicity
In dedication to the temple
We find a common language
in the photos we take together

On to the next big temple
Where Thay tells of no more anger
I like the simple one best
where joy of life shines bright

1 April 2005 – More
Binh Dinh Province Temples

Yellow fields –
Cone hatted harvesters
stoop, slowly reap
Palm trees sway

Narrow homes
line the road
Balcony atop
new second floor

Peasant homes
have pointed roofs
tin, ceramic tile
vegetable garden

Eucalyptus
unexpected
Farming ducks
out to graze

Temple, Museum to King,
who fought back Chinese
I retreat from sun, marshal arts
into shade by pond

Water ripples
Trees reflect
I recline
toward sleep

There in half state
Message is clear
Build inner practice
the only way to help

2 April 2005 – Qui Nhon, Binh Dinh

Walking meditation
with Vietnamese
Temple robed
new friends

Thay teaches them the way
with wide smile and love
Quietly we walk together
hundreds in mindfulness

Thay says take the vow
When we see energy
of anger arising
don't do, say anything

We don't want to hurt
ourselves or others
Breathe, do walking med
Irritation subsides

The hall is packed
with grey-robed Vietnamese
He teaches Buddha psychology
as he does in the West

Each Buddhist practitioner
to help raise awareness
needs to practice mindful
breathing and walking

Monastics or lay
We need to know how
to generate mindfulness –
Lay people should practice, too

In mindfulness we discover
real reason, not other person,
why seed of inner anger
has grown so very big

We become anger victims
Anger grows in society
Family should tell each other
Don't water my anger seeds

In the last ten years
seeds of anger watered
Now we use this trip
to forgive beyond anger

Transform not to spread
this anger within
Remember other person
still living in hell

So we come back
to be able to help
other person transform
as victim of own anger

Our desire to help
Our anger transformed
changed into love
Western Buddhists learnt

What do Vietnamese think
used to other Buddhist practice?
Thay tells them to go home
and try these techniques

Mostly in the Temple
older women sit
They smile when Thay says
They may feel anger at spouse

He tells of peace treaty
to practice in 24 hours
Write it on a card
New idea to carry round

I can't help but wonder
how Vietnamese audience
feel about Thay's talk
So different than devotion

Chau says her relatives
who heard Thay in Hanoi
thought that he made sense
Bringing Buddhism into life

3 April 2005 – Qui Nhon, Binh Dinh

Today Thay talks
of culture change
from extended family
to globalized way

In audience now
teenagers appear
listening attentively
to Grandfather Zen Master

He tells of past families
of four generations
all living together
of space for kids to play

Thay surprises them
telling of Western discontent
Money can't buy happiness
Consumerism false god

Family communication
Democratic decisions
Understanding one another
The key to Vietnam's future

Two roots of Vietnam
The family and Temple
Need happiness in both
Individualism, Responsibility

Vietnamese friend tells
of practitioners' happiness
to have Westerners here
Never imagined Western Buddhists

In today's walking med
Vietnamese are quieter
Even the hall is still
Mindful energy spreads

In just two days
people from the district
coming as far as Hue
have opened to mindful way

They come to hold my hand
Take pictures with us galore
Smile when I say hello
Are happy to see us here

In English Touching Earth
Sister Susan guides us through
I feel the box round my heart
disintegrate into Temple floor

Touching reconciliation
possibilities unbelieved
If Vietnam can heal
so can my heart

Nhu says her cousins
hearing Thay in Binh Dinh
so happy to breathe, walk
learning mindful way

Before they only knew
bowing in the Temple
reading Thay's book
they want to practice

Everywhere I go
here in Saigon
people know of Thay
want to hear of his trip

Conditions so ripe
for reconciliation
seeing this healing
gives me such courage

21 April 2005

REPORTING BACK TO SANGHA

Returning to Temple of Phuong's living room
Touching the earth of their carpeted floor
Being once again with Cambridge Sangha
feeling collective mindful vibration

Remembering I'm a being of light
Feeling straightness of spine
Seeing parent's true intension
naming me to bring happiness

I tell of amazement
that no Vietnamese
showed anger at all
towards visiting Americans

Phuong explains Vietnamese culture
having survived centuries of war
means people quickly rebuild
not grasping past war in mind

Freed from past dread
how light one can be
forgiveness easier flow
so I try the same

So much to learn
from my dear friends
Vietnamese offer me
opportunity for release

*Experience of having a Reiki
empowerment*

28 April 2005

Green iridescent light
glowing in my hands
as I'm re-attuned

Radiance spreads
into my heart
expanding to body

Grant me my love
acceptance as I am
smiling to faults

Touching my ease
just where I left it
in blossoming life

Now as you spread
filling inner body
mind can recede

Once cleansed
green glow
expands out

2 May 2005

Remembering Mom saying
she wanted to live on
to work on herself
in order to help others

Now I see more clearly
just what she meant
as I build inner light
shining out

Last night reciting
14 Mindfulness Trainings
with Order Sangha
feeling power

Thinking of touching
meaning more deeply
living simpler
as our lives change

Bob and I in new time
shifting toward essence
his travelling adventure
both building inner life

Separate and together
each taking care of self
as best way to insure
taking care of each other

11 June 2005

Forgiveness miracle
reconciliation
possible when moving
toward love unity

Allowing time
for conditions to ripen
each to learn
their own lessons

Moving toward miracles
purifying mind/heart
allows for possibility
of miracles to happen

2 July 2005

BOB'S COLLEGE RETIREMENT PARTY

Death disruption of train
Unexpected life reminder
Sending Reiki compassion

Yet why today
Bob's leaving do
We must arrive

His speech to deliver
Resolution ceremony
starting without him

Resonating his dream
trying to reach party
unable to arrive

Finally we find taxi
ringing Kev with update
smiling to startling stress

Body parts on track
Short life perspective
Strange concurrence

Coalescing of change
long threatened, awaited
Surprising to suddenly happen

Shift so abrupt, yet slow
Anger mellowed by heart
maturing into compassion

Wisdom from brave Bob
seeing beyond division
staff, managers both people

Leaving with clear focus
of value in the students
Refugees our teachers

Respect bringing unity
No need for John's anger
Bob releasing to own power

I see my confused loyalty
to John, true justice fighter
Yet over the top through anger

Bob has more perspective
That's why he's ready to go
while I'll be staying on

*Sharing my Vietnam slides with my
Sangha*

16 July 2005

Being spirit of lightness
letting heaviness fade
in openhearted laughter

How sweet life can be
allowing sadness to pass
touching natural joy

To offer buoyant bliss
must nurture in myself
happiness ancestors want

Crown receiving light
third eye seeing beauty
throat singing out poems

Heart opening to joy
solar plexus accepting me
belly digesting healing

Being with Cambridge Sangha
warm without grasping
resonating at different levels

Culture, personality affect
but Sangha energy connects
through vibration of practice

Some easier friendship
all friends through practice
as in International Sangha

Showing Vietnam slides
bringing Sangha into home
laughing with Phuong and Phouc

Sharing Vietnam journey
with understanding Sangha
spreads Thay's seeds

23 August 2005

Sweet heart connection
to Helena
live art performer
mother to be
of my grandchild

Cooking for me
I see her costumes
visuals in progress
hear her script
and share Reiki

Renewed from holiday
at ease with self
facing downpour
desk not of choosing
with easy acceptance

Yet with trust
working with colleagues
of long connection
timetable, new office
shaping up well

On to Helena
Reiki sent ahead
goodwill both sides
such easy rapport
sweet heart connection

Our meeting
still so new
yet with feeling
of old link
through essence

I feel so lucky
my life can change
Changing my perspective
releasing resistance
allowing easy flow

Oh what beauty
red ripe berries
birds with song
Kev, Helena with baby
me with sweet Bob

9 September 2005

Marilyn made me laugh
in the midst of having Reiki
Startling the silence
hooting from my depths

Feeling her presence
once more on couch
with Liz and I
remembering her

Her pleasant
composed solidity
honest poise
respecting all

Casual manner
friendly way
Spiritual growth
as she matured

Earlier days
back at St Matthew's
anti racist/sexist
affecting school

Later her advice
on Women's Studies
Friendly encounters
meeting by river

When we last met
at Reiki Refresher
struck by how well
taking care of herself

Removing her wig
exposing spiky orange
her illness too
a part of her growth

Giving her Reiki
feeling sacred being
what great strides
along her path

Now her body's gone
I still feel her ease
smiling I sense
her joining in Reiki

Her gentle touch
I well remember
but giving Reiki
needs no body

She's doing the feet
as I Reiki Liz
On my turn
heart sprouts laughter

Yes I see
you are released
radiating ease
sparks my heart

After Marilyn's death touching Reiki
principle of accepting blessings that
we discussed together with Rahelly

10 September 2005

Rekindling life's romance
freshness after the rain
sacred after her death
footsteps touch the earth
with my guiding breath

Vivid green
bright red berry
Smiling to open
inner essence
rekindled out

Resistance noted
seen, accepted
seeking rut
no longer needed
accepting blessings

24 September 2005

Healing past hurt
with Reiki love-light
Anger directed at me
creating confusion, fear

Metal plate protection
sealing off my heart
Seeing babyhood anew
father's hurt as well

Sending healing back
transforming our old pain
Allowing me the chance
to begin afresh

Less drive to hearken back
to safety of rut pain
Victim of little use
harmony so much better

No need for hardened mould
release through loving hurt
Vibration higher now
when I touch, breathe peace

Valuing me
believing in power
to protect myself
with mindful awareness

Cold toxic release
allows rejuvenation
into childbirth project
where I want to go

23 December 2005

True Wonderful Commitment
first of all for me
loving myself in the eye
accepting what I see

Deep in winter's chill
inner warmth burns through
connection to Reiki current
building inner patience

Savouring this calm /stillness
allowing me freedom
from 'shoulds' and driving on
when there is only now

The unknown future
of which I worry
is basically made up
of cumulative nows

This moment of calm
brings me closer
to future composed
of built up peace

With solidity
I cope better
with whatever
future brings

With wisdom
detachment stronger
intelligent compassion
presence of awareness

Allowing loved ones own story
nourishing my serenity
The torch when bright
naturally shines out

True Wonderful Commitment
to my life force
interconnected to all
through universal web

26 January 2006

Touching Jewish roots
There what will I find?
Beneath anger, shame
the warm hug of home

Parents, ancestors
holding me tight
laughing loudly
gesturing wildly

What kind of a place is this England?
What's wrong with arguing, shouting?
Why box in all your emotions
hiding in false politeness?

Always the same assumption
this being a Christian land
where so many others live
as 'other', stranger at home

I want to strengthen my roots
to feel Jewish stability
below the shouting exists
solidity of 5000 years

Yet my roots go deeper
back to Goddess worship
Great Earth Mother
the Tree of Jezebel

Seeing Jewish suppression
of my shining roots
feeling witchly pagan
I want to reject the Jew

Then I reject myself
That's so easy to do
So let me look again
Take what is useful to me

After meeting newborn Ella at home
with her parents

22 February 2006

Baby Ella
White fluffy
pure energy
in my arms

Yes, just what I wanted
glow to light the way
giving death perspective
Beauty of this moment

Feeling our deep bond
link to ancestor's eyes
combined with Walsh chin
to make new generation

And our babies once
now become the parents
Smiling to sweet couple
taking up the challenge

Oh, what wondrous feel
flow of life's sweet milk
hope's regeneration
Cries keep us in now

1 March 2006

Babysitting Ella
Perfect newborn baby
miniature ear, fingers
almond family eyes
dating back centuries
back to mother Russia

Sweet Helena Mama
feeding her own milk
to Ella already growing
in this special week
Miracle of life
shared with Papa Kev

Jazzy background music
relaxes Ella so
With a name like that
what else can you expect?
Daddy flies her round
Mummy talks so sweetly

Together they entrust
this new generation
to her grandparents
who watch her sleep and smile
First time out alone
'Best pint in years'

Of course, she also wakes
crying as she's walked
that's to be expected
Still the glow remains
as we cherish this
first time alone with Ella

After returning from Sister Eleni's
Scottish retreat

15 March 2006

Dear sweet, precious Joy
feeding consciousness
nurturing seeds
to help my heart open

Shock of seeing
base negativity
background presence
holding me back

As eating healthy food
my consciousness too
needs to be fed
self appreciation

In that value
my precious being
reverberates deeply
'is' the universe

Habit from birth
being reversed
so sweet baby Ella
can grow openhearted

And I can be
more fully alive
tasting my sweetness
brings sweetness to life

True Wonderful Commitment
to water my consciousness
so positive seeds
can flower divine

3 May 2006

Kevin Kangaroo
Ella in his pouch
legs dangling
eyes bright
Watching

Four eyes from two
there at heart centre
new blue gaze
intently taking in
colour, light, wonder

Kevin, too, gains vision
seeing beyond the mask
to where happiness lies
deepening understanding
enjoying family life

8 June 2006

ELLAVISION

Seeing through Ella eyes
where light and colour thrill
without mind interference

Enjoying green swaying shapes
without knowing their names
or caring to qualify or judge

Refreshing glimpse
beyond busy mind spin
that keeps me from truly seeing

Here in this moment
light green elation
nothing left to fear

Resting ego mind
for wider connection
allowing doubt to ease

Big me being
part of garden
one with earth

After reading transmission poems of the 8 generations of the
Lieu Quan Dharma Line and connecting to the 42 generations
of the Lam Te Dhyana School into which I'd been ordained

11 June 11 2006

I. Smile

Smile, release
Inner smile
deep in belly
Buddha nature

Buried by
worry, fear
I breathe in
glimpsing grin

Then I see
belly smile
radiate
to heart, mind

More powerful than
physical smile
aiming down
at my belly

Through the fog
of worry, fear
smile seen/felt
from Tantien

II. Release

Allowing judges
out through skin
opening pores
letting go

Letting go
of worry plans
breathing out
fog of fear

What a relief
concentration
of spiritual ancestor
with piercing eyes

III. Smile, Release

In aware state
touching transmission
forty-third generation
spirit in me

Breathing into
Tantien smile
breathing out
confusion fog

Working through
allowing goodness
in consciousness
to feed smile

17 June 2006

MOM FEEDS ELLA

Feeding granddaughter Ella
looking down at my hand
there I see my Mom's

Yes, she's feeding you
sweet baby continuation
of our ancestral line

Mom feeds you with love
smiling her serenity
holding your new born body

All my past generations
echo across time to say
'Ve just vant you to be happy!

'Mazel tov on your birth
your smile and Elllavision
Use them in good health!'

Mulling college retirement in
half sleep brings clarity

8 July 2006

After college
dense green
square mist
brings trust

Teaching Reiki
path opening
energy guiding
steps mindful

Letting go control
yellow solar plexus
way to orange smile
coming into own

Bright stars
bursting through
black sky
bringing light

ELLA'S NAMING CEREMONY

Watching Ella with Joanne
we chat as she smiles in cot
Feeding her together
joyful at her growth

Wheeling Ella to party
created by her parents
with much preparation
power of their creation

Involving family, friends
creating community
in which Ella basks
in joint celebration

Puppet shows and jokes
meanings of her name
magic and dance
heart-felt words

Irish contingent
with hearts so warm
helping Ella touch
the Blarney Stone

'Lechayim!'
from Jewish line
sending stories, poems
with our good wishes

My heart so wide with 'naches'
from Kevin and his baby
beautiful, bright partner
blessed by their creations

Mingling of friends
from Kev, Helena's past
Art College days
to their London group

Hearts open wide
to take in new life
The one, the only
Ella Walsh Biderman

Held up to the sky
as we shout her name
she grins ear to ear
taking in the vibs

May blue sky protect her
sun shine down upon her
keeping eyes, smile wide
bringing love to earth

After returning from Wales where Bob and I meandered together,
touching hearts, I prepare to camp in Plum Village, with mixed
emotions coming up to view.

15 August 2006

Trusting process
Trusting self
knowing I'm more
when I open to see

I am my teachers
back to Yen Tu
peaceful stability
in midst of war

Thay, Sister Jina
there within me
and my mindfulness
to represent them

I am my parents
grandparents, beyond
Jewish ancestors'
zest for life

I am the wind
swaying the trees
purple flowers
red berries for birds

I am my angst
deep inside
and the balance
of Reiki symbol

I am my fear
of being a healer
and the healer
smiling back to me

I am the confidence
that I so need
to move beyond
failure/success

Coming into
third age phase
I am the one
I've been seeking

28 August 2006

PLUM VILLAGE RETURN

Coming home
with mixed emotions
longing but dread
of difficult last visit

Bringing loved-one
in time of distress
illness continues
in three week stay

I book to go home
to Lower Hamlet
after realising
fear's kept me away

Such difficulties
embarrassment
pain of loved-one
I want to save

Sisters accepting
beauty surround
let her be
but breakdown persists

Thay looks and speaks
of intelligent compassion
father goes away
so children can grow

In the end
we have to leave
though deep love
brings some clarity

Two years later
after illness accepted
I return alone
to transform seeds

Healing energy
in plant surround
Thay's insights
sisters' smiles

Walking, sitting
sleeping on the earth
being Order Member
laughing, sharing

Stepping back
into house of our stay
defiled, immaculate
one in the same

There in my depths
transformation
I am not separate
my karma collective

Staying in present
each step touches home
childhood joy
springs up anew

Surroundings so vivid
once I let go
three dimensional
beauty in bush

RETURNING HOME

My beloved gem
propelling practice
ever richer
into awareness

Dear loved-one
allowing me
to deeply taste
suffering, ultimate

Colours so vivid
red and purple
green leaves
waving in wind

Beyond flatness
three dimensions
there in depth
bird flaps her wings

You and I
walk together
my anger gone
I synchronise our steps

Feeling earth
and my breath
you tell of blue sky
and her beauty

Walking together
with my gem
life is wondrous
just as it is

13 September 2006

Heaven in a little park
Red flowers and tree
overhanging bench

Us below
three generations
feeding Ella

Carrot and milk
life's sweet essence
alive in us all

Taking it in turns
Mama, Dada, Nan
helping Ella grow

She helps us grow
deepening heart
connecting to childhood

Oh, sweet quiet park
warmth of us together
island of family peace

28 September 2006

THAY'S BIRTHDAY PROMISE

My dear, dear teacher
I want to honour you
on your eightieth birthday
with the gift you asked

A small token
for all you've taught
helped me to touch
and understand

I worry I won't be perfect
in keeping this promise
Then laugh out loud
smile to my old habit

I see you in me
just as you said
and ask you to help
me keep my promise

I thought about eating
I do say short gatha
but such distraction
with family and friends

Breakfast came to mind
Mostly I eat alone
No one else to blame
for my wandering mind

So I tried it this morning
guarding my mind closely
Then I had to smile
at trying too hard

So dear Thay, Sangha
I make you this promise
to mindfully eat breakfast
and smile at wandering mind

I wish you happy birthday
your continuation blooms
expanding in my heart
leaves swaying in the wind

30 September 2006

Ancient desire
reminded by friend
being dharma teacher
in publishing poems

Beyond scaring myself
going back to bed for safety
healing more deeply
what old poems resurface

Embarrassment of new ones
still so imperfect
Laughing out loud
dear sweet illusion

Notion of perfection
idea of saving all
ego aggrandising
disempowering

As with my baby picture
I'm neither the same
nor completely different
somewhere in-between

Middle way so clear
easy beyond notions
touching Thay in me
ripe berries on tree

Absolutes drop away
as leaves sway in breeze
branches three dimensional
I am the same

Rounded, multicoloured
in sun and shade
patterns of shadows
ever-changing

After our regular Wednesday evening Sangha meditation,
a friend shared that he'd come face to face with his tiger.
We'd both spoken about working with our fear. The next
morning, after meditating, I wrote this poem for us.

5 October 2006

Face to face with the tiger
She shows herself to me
There's no judgement, anger
nose and mouth just be

I smile and look her in the eyes
She looks back in mirror clarity
I breathe and she does the same
She is but a part of me

I feel her in solar plexus
She feels me in universe surround
What is there to fear?
Suddenly she smiles

22 October 2006 – Nafplio, Greece

Cypress tree
before orange mount
grey streaks
flowing down

Turquoise sea
hitting rocks
woosh, woosh
white foam

Me floating
on diamond waves
one with all
laughing with Julia

24 October 2006 – Myceane, Greece

Mother Goddess
atop Myceane
flowing orange
down to me

Eat my child
enjoy my bounty
taste tomato
breathe in past

I'm still here
atop the ruins
you can feel me
beyond violent myths

Trading, farming
cooperative acts
lentils, grains
olive oil in pots

Female figures
of earthen clay
adorn graves
and daily life

Between the mounts
in silent splendour
unperturbed
I nurture on

Sleeping near Acropolis after crowded visit

27 October 2006 – Athens

Floating dream
above Acropolis
Heal thyself
with sacred stone

Resonating there
beyond time
monuments grand
sacrifices awful

Heal thyself
by letting go
of idea of future
you make/decide

The route barred
from walking on mount
is what brings
flying to mind

Oh, freedom
lightness of joy
in dreams so rare
weightless flow

There in essence
of white glow
all is well
Athena smiles

27 October 2006 – Athens

JEWISH MUSEUM

I see relatives
in the photos
Auschwitz transport
identity cards

Centuries of ease
co-existence
one hundred thousand
Jews in Greece

Half in Salonica
before the war
All gone now
I want to cry

But I'm touched
by Greek resistance
Archbishop, police
citizens protest

I send Reiki
to striped camp suit
woven jacket
that saved survivor

I want to cry
but hear again
We want you to be happy
that's transformation way

Jews in resistance
hidden in mountains
villagers, families
escaping to Turkey

Yet as war ends
almost all dead
I want to cry
but no tears come

I tell museum lady
how lucky I feel
our eyes meet
in depth of knowing

5 November 2006

Safe in bed
warm in rainbow
It doesn't matter
which poems go in book

What matters is this acceptance
enjoying day with daughter
breathing down to safety
smiling at wandering mind

For Sue, Sheila and Claudie

15 November 2006

WOMEN'S LIB SUPPER

Meeting beyond time
with such old friends
Slipping into patterns
and moving beyond
to heart core
where we touch

CLEANSING RENEWAL

Yearly haircut
snipping off pain
of past terrors
swept away
in fluff mound
for new beginning

Hair wash massage
Staring into mirror
find power eye and sad
Reiking them both
Enjoying Franco energy
cutting with care

Talk of Buddhist Temple
then we slip into
hair cutting meditation
focused, even snips
Relaxed, peaceful
cleansing renewal

Oh, what lightness
joyful blow dry
changing the part
turning ends under
final cream
See you next year

Out I glide
feeling a million
to Kilburn High Road
where world hurries by
I settle into Nero
to watch it all pass

22 November 2006

'I am enthusiastic about life'
Kerin's affirmation for me
A gift I've always wanted
her giving spiritual presence

Kerin, perfect daughter for me
allowing such opportunity
for my sacred growth
so I may become who I am

Kerin, so special, unique
allowing for world view shifts
Forcing me to look again
to see life's deeper truths

Thank you, darling daughter
for that moment together
as we repeat as one
'I am enthusiastic about life'

7 December 2006

Mom within
every cell
of my body
smiling to me

Mom approving
serenely pleased
of my way
learning through life

My heart open
letting in light
to shine beyond
need to defend

Letting go
even deeper
of that victim
justified

Sweet freedom
laughing out loud
so much better
than my frown

Misperceptions
oh so easy
just as easy
to release

So dear Mom
I let you go
to grow myself
You smile within

You want me to grow
beyond leaning on you
into spiritual being
touching inner glow

My own light
beam of cosmos
shine of whole
reflecting back

Dear sweet Mom
I heal myself
healing my daughter
ancestor guilt

You are so wise
to let me go
on my own path
while ever present

I know you're here
for Susan too
loving us both
as two hands

No competition
each so different
no bad/good
Just lighting way

18 December 2006

Wondrous weekend
children, offspring
each growing positive
in their own way

Good intensions
all around
build sweetness
of family love

Chanukah candles
shining bright
ancestors smile
latkes delight

12 January 2007

Finding old drawings
tucked in sketch book
of nineteen eighty

Houseplant studies
with three year old
Kevin baby boy

Drawing of him
wrapped in my hair
flower opened heart

Family at crossroads
future unimaginable
starting with change

Puppet Centre demise
depressing let down
the way to wonder

Writing, travelling
new life ahead
by releasing old

Barely remember
houseplant looking
such free drawing

On such pleasure
in rediscovery
of flowing lines

Twenty seven years later
unthinkable use
in Dharma diary book

Come so far
by letting go
allowing new